"A full stop he'
heart and soul':
experience in se
of all. She wall
her bright and l .... authenticity of rare
depth. I wholeheartedly encourage you to join in her
magic!"

Marité Hagman, MPH, *Whole Health* Program
Manager, University of Wisconsin;
Advanced Energy Healer

"There is a special form of wisdom which can come
through a young person who, in one shocking moment, is
no longer young. Such a transmutation of sorrow is not
always assured as it is the vulnerable sibling of despair. It
is from this tender and shaky edge that Laura speaks to
us with a bright and grounded faith in the possibility of
being made whole by committing oneself to a path of well-
being. We are all messy miracles, but we can find our way
if we follow her example by committing to such a path of
mindful, diligent, clear care. This is where the magic
happens."

Flint Sparks, Zen Teacher, Former
Clinical Psychologist

"Laura writes from a place of tenderhearted compassion
and wisdom. *The Magic of Well-Being* gently welcomes the
reader to ponder life's big questions, get to know
themselves better, and achieve inner peace. It's like
receiving a big, warm, hug from a dear friend."

Kristy Wessel, Librarian, Lover of
Cat Memes, Mom

"*The Magic of Well-Being* was such a fun and insightful book to read. I found a beautiful balance of masterful teachings, presented in tangible ways, and filled with imagery and storytelling. I recommend curling up with a hot beverage and preparing yourself for a gentle, Soul opening ride with this beautiful book."

Emily Moody, Owner EMbody'd Work, LMT, CR,
CST, RYT, Soul Art™ Guide

"*The Magic of Well-Being* isn't about creating a bigger and better life, or a single formula to finding happiness. Well-being is what we already have once we stop resisting our life and start living it. There is something freeing and almost Zen-like about accepting that family and home life doesn't have to be anything other than what it is: a little messy, a little imperfect, but at its essence, exactly what it needs to be. Laura Thomas doesn't take her readers on a journey, instead she walks alongside readers as a friend willing to share and receive the wisdom that is already contained within."

Hilary Novacek Bundt, Licensed Social Worker,
Educator, Mom

THE MAGIC OF WELL-BEING

A Modern Guide to Lasting Happiness

Laura Thomas

ISBN-978-1-7341717-1-6

Cover design by Book Cover Ideas
Book design and layout by Sarah Elle Studio

Cedar & Sage Press
Colorado, USA

For Flint Sparks—my teacher, my friend

INTRODUCTION

The odds of being born are very, very small. It's impossible to conceive of all the factors that came together throughout history so that we could be here. All of the people who found each other, the challenges they overcame, the timing of big events.

To be gifted life is, quite literally, a miracle. Magic, even.

And yet, despite our great fortune, many of us are unhappy.

Not an obvious unhappiness. It's subtle. A feeling that things aren't as they should be. A low-level malaise that leads us to wonder if the next best thing is just around the corner, when life is different, or better. When *we* are different, or better.

For a long time, this was my experience. I felt like a victim of life. Things happened "to me"–or didn't happen to me–and my self-worth was dependent on external events going a certain way.

If I receive this award, then I'll feel confident. If I get a boyfriend, I'll finally feel attractive.

But no matter how many outward goals I achieved, there was always something else, another bargain I tried making with life. Another reason why I couldn't be happy with things as they were.

In 2011, I reached a turning point. After experiencing a shattering tragedy, I finally woke up to how I was living. I didn't like what I saw. I wasn't kind to myself. My thoughts were often negative, and I purposefully played small, feeling unworthy of happiness and love.

Sometimes tragedy flips our world on its head, and from that vantage point, we see the things we were once blind to. We see a fundamental pain that we finally want to address. Not because we feel brave and strong, but because we don't think we can keep living the way we have been.

This different vantage point—and a touch of desperation—fostered a new curiosity about my life. Did I want to continue playing small when my heart longed to do things that frightened me, like write books? Why did I think I was unworthy of love when I would never think that about someone else?

Could I actually find a way to be the person I wanted to be, someone who was resilient, who supported herself, and who didn't wish to be different?

My curiosity opened doors. I began meditating and going on silent retreats. I read books about mindfulness and yoga, becoming a student of my heart, mind, and body. In many ways, I committed my life to exploring what it means to be human. Slowly, I felt my perspective shift. I started to see a way to be happy without making bargains with life. I started to see choices where I had thought none existed.

The deeper I dove, the more life lessons popped up in meditation settings and traditional wisdom teachings, but also in more contemporary sources, like Harry Potter and fashion icons. Uncovering a different way of living was magical. Not because it transported me to a fanciful place where life finally went the way I wanted, but because it drew me deeper into the life I was living and asked me to see the magic that was already there.

I wrote this book because sometimes life is hard. We feel challenged, and we don't know what to do, or where to turn. I get it. I feel it, too. Inside this book are the most powerful tools and insights

I've discovered on my journey. They help me feel a little more stable when my world is rocked. They soothe my heart when I'm overwhelmed. Most importantly, they've helped me craft a life where happiness isn't fleeting—it's lasting.

I don't own this wisdom. It is age-old and threaded through many ancient traditions. The challenging thing with wisdom is it can feel inaccessible at times, so I put a modern spin on it. I believe that, more than ever, we need to look backwards to mindfully move forwards. We need ancient wisdom to find lasting happiness in our modern world.

I want to share these insights with you so that you can walk this journey with me, gently. These are learned skills. Ease and happiness are possible, if we're willing to do the work. If we're willing to practice again and again, and forgive ourselves for our mistakes along the way.

I believe well-being is the most magical thing on the planet. Once you start looking, you'll see magic everywhere. In big life events, like marriage or promotions or the arrival of a baby, but also in small moments that only we see. There's magic in forgiving yourself. There's magic in pausing to watch a flock of birds soar through the sky in their instinctive formation. There's magic in saying *yes* to your life, even if when it's hard. Because even our challenges can be a doorway into appreciating all that we have.

There is magic in each moment, if we're open to it. I hope you are. I hope we can explore the magic of well-being together as we learn how to embrace life fully, starting now.

THE MAGIC OF WELL-BEING

A Modern Guide to Lasting Happiness

BOOK ONE

WELL-BEING

The Quiet Art of Embracing Life

Of course it is happening inside your head,
Harry, but why on earth should that mean
that it is not real?

–Albus Dumbledore

THE BATTLE

Without knowing it, we walk around armed. Each morning, as we don our clothes for the day and make coffee, we prepare other, invisible things.

Weapons.

The purpose of our weapons: to resist life.

How we use them: any way we can.

We attack, edit, bury, and ambush. We threaten and cajole, seeking to manipulate life into being exactly what we want. Some unconscious part of us believes that if we put up enough resistance, life will finally provide the things we've determined will bring us happiness.

Money. Relationships. Status. Balance. Perfection. Success.

Only when our requests have been fulfilled will be put down our weapons and just live.

But life hasn't complied yet, so we release another battle cry and charge back onto the field.

Never truly able to rest. Never truly satisfied with things as they are.

It's not our fault. This battle rages unconsciously. But it's critical that we bring it to our attention, because there's a problem with this approach—a flaw in the premise, and it will always prevent us from achieving the lasting happiness we desire.

Life isn't meant to be fought. It is meant to be lived, as if it were the greatest gift we've ever been handed.

ANOTHER WAY

When we resist life, we never feel whole. We don't trust that our existence is meaningful and worthy, just as it is. We think we need to be *different*, *better*, or *more*.

This is a trap. There is no such thing as different or better or more. There is only here, now.

There is only us in this moment. If we don't learn how to embrace our life fully, no amount of yoga pants or Brené Brown talks will recover the wholeness we believe has been lost.

But it hasn't been lost. We are *already* whole, we are *already* worthy. And nothing in the expansive universe can take that away.

We just need to learn how to see it.

WELL-BEING

There is another option. A way to bypass the battle completely and finally experience lasting happiness.

It's called *well-being*.

Well-being isn't related to physical fitness or optimized nutrition. It is a state of being; a way to live the life we want now, without equivocation.

In *The Lord of the Rings*, Frodo laments to Gandalf that he wishes his life had been different.

"I wish the ring had never come to me. I wish none of this had happened," he says.

Gandalf responds, "So do all who live to see such times. But that is not for them to decide. All we have to decide is what to do with the time that is given to us."

When we live in well-being, our happiness isn't dependent on external circumstances. We put down our weapons and start embracing life not as we think it should be, but as it *is*. We start deciding what to do with the time that is given to us.

WELL-BEING IS LIKE

A RIVERBED

Well-being is like a wide channel through which our life flows. It's big enough to hold all of our experiences, including our highs and lows, and everything in between, without judgment or resistance.

It's like a riverbed—mostly unseen, but critically important. The riverbed provides a welcoming container for all of life, and as a rule, it doesn't eject anything out. In fact, each component held within the riverbed is seen as necessary—as part of creating the larger picture. The curling eddies, the fish hovering at the sides, the debris floating downstream—they all belong inside the riverbed.

Well-being is the same. When we're in our riverbed of well-being, we become big enough to hold everything with the courage to say, "I am willing for all of this to be my life."

WHEN WE AREN'T

IN WELL-BEING

Rivers are dynamic. They can be flat and calm, or steep and churning; they can support tiny freshwater snails, and transport large logs.

Life is also dynamic. Sometimes things are seamless and easeful, and other times everything crashes down around us—or inside of us.

To be in our riverbed of well-being is to have a certain relationship with life's inevitable ups and downs: we choose to be bigger than any one experience, and we embrace all of life from a place of acceptance and appreciation, rather than victimization and blame.

When we *aren't* in our riverbed of well-being, we're in the river, subjected to its whims and changes. When we're in the rapids, we experience nothing but the rapids as we struggle to keep our head above the frothing water. Similarly, certain experiences in life can drown out everything else. An angry response can consume us, causing harm to ourselves and others. Fear can overwhelm us, keeping us from stepping into the unknown of a relationship or a dream. Jealousy strips away joy, leaving us bitter and closed-hearted.

Being in the river makes life tough.

Even calm waters can be deceptive if we're in the river. We think we've overcome all obstacles and life will be smooth sailing from here. Inevitably, at some point, we hit another rough patch of water, and we're again lost in hardship.

Happiness is fleeting in the river. It depends on the things we encounter, and it comes and goes with the calm waters. But when we're in our riverbed of well-being, happiness is lasting. We're bigger than every obstacle. We're stable throughout the storms. Nothing inside the river can disrupt our steadiness.

The riverbed doesn't control what passes through its container, but it can hold all of life with ease.

RESISTING LIFE:

AN EXAMPLE

There's a good reason we resist aspects of our life. They're painful. Uncomfortable. Why on earth would we stop fighting them? Worse, why would we *embrace* a reality we don't desire?

When I was 23, a recent college graduate, grief sat heavy on my heart. Six months prior, my only brother had been lost to suicide.

With every fiber of my being I resisted that reality.

Scott was my older brother, my best friend. With every day that passed without him, I felt nausea digging into my gut and panic igniting my blood. *No no no! It's not supposed to be like this. He's supposed to be here with me, tackling me into the couch with that teasing glint in his eyes.*

I would never see that glint—or those eyes—again. It was unacceptable, too painful, and I fought back against my life, weapons blazing.

Resistance can take many forms. It can exist in the negative things we say to ourselves, or the emotions we don't allow ourselves to feel. Like grief. Resistance is the subtle way we express, "I am *not* willing for all of this to be my life."

It took a while for the consequences of my resistance to take hold, and it was at that point, six months later, that I started to see: I wasn't healing. No—things were breaking down. My body was wasting away, my heart closed against new relationships. Even my mind struggled, forgetting what someone told me minutes after our conversation. I wasn't moving forward, stuck scrambling back to an unreachable past.

Unknowingly, I had created an internal barrier. There was a wall separating the life I wanted to keep living as a family of four from my reality of a family of three. In that reality were all sorts of emotions I didn't want to feel, because if I actually allowed my grief and agony in, I feared I'd never recover. I'd become too lost, too broken, to find my way back to myself. Would I even *want* to find my way back if Scott was gone?

Resisting life was easier than embracing it. For a time, at least.

Traumas have their own healing process, and everyone's is different. On my journey, I finally got to a point where my internal barrier was keeping me from health and happiness. With such a big divide, half of my life was on either side, and I became half a person. I couldn't do it any longer, and I knew Scott wouldn't have wanted that existence for me. Deep down, *I* didn't want that for me.

Just surviving, not thriving.

Even though it was frightening, I started wondering what my options were. Could a different approach lead to the peace I wanted so badly? Not because I kept resisting my life, but because I started embracing it, grief and fear and heartache and all?

RESISTANCE

IN THE LITTLE THINGS

R esistance doesn't only happen in large life events. It also happens in small, everyday things. Little ways in which we create internal barriers between what is, and what we think should be.

We resist our body's need for rest and recovery by pounding caffeine all day.

We resist anxiety and stress by buying new clothes to feel that brief high.

We resist our feelings of inadequacy by scrolling through social media, which, incidentally, makes us feel more inadequate.

It's not bad to have preferences for how we want life to go. But true happiness doesn't depend on things going the way we want. It depends on how we relate to what's already happening.

Are we resisting life, or are we embracing it?

POOH,

THE WELL-BEING MASTER

Winnie the Pooh got stuck in Rabbit's hole after eating one too many pawfuls of honey. He was upset for a bit. "Oh bother," he said. He even shed a tear at his predicament. Then he accepted his uncomfortable circumstance, asking his friends to read to him until he became thin enough for the bottom half of his body to rejoin the top.

Rabbit used Pooh's rear end as a clothing rack. Christopher Robin indulged Pooh with books. Pooh fasted, until, at the end of the week, he was heaved by a long line of forest critters and *pop!* he was free!

Pooh smiled, nodded thanks, and ambled off to find his next adventure with a soft hum, leaving Christopher Robin to muse our favorite endearing phrase: "Silly old bear."

And thus, Pooh demonstrated well-being: a willingness to embrace all of life, both when it goes our way, and when it doesn't. When things are easy, and when they're hard. Even when our challenges are of our own making.

Pooh was able to be in his riverbed of well-being, wide enough to hold all of his experiences without judgment or resistance.

ATTITUDE PROBLEM

Well-being doesn't fix problems. It's not a magic pill that makes all our hardships disappear.

In fact, well-being doesn't see life as a problem that needs to be fixed. It doesn't think our lives are broken, defective, or unfortunate, no matter how many troubles we face.

In the words of Captain Jack Sparrow, "The problem is not the problem. The problem is your attitude about the problem."

Well-being is an invitation to change our attitude towards life. To put our weapons down and open to the gifts in each moment, even if they weren't the ones we requested.

THE BEDROCK

Being human comes with a few truths:
We have very little control.

We never have all the answers.

Everything changes.

We will lose everything we love.

Or, as Jennifer Welwood so poignantly says in her poem *The Dakini Speaks*, "Impermanence is life's only promise to us, and she keeps it with ruthless impeccability."

And the final truth: despite all of that, lasting happiness is possible.

These truths are the bedrock from which our riverbed is carved. We don't get to choose the layers, or how the material came together, but they create the larger context of our existence.

When we acknowledge these truths, our riverbed can hold anything, and we can truly flourish.

INVITING MARA TO TEA

There's a Buddhist story about the demon god Mara.

Mara represents all the things we don't like about our lives. The things we want to resist.

Every time Mara appeared at the Buddha's door, the Buddha made a unique choice. Instead of slamming the door in Mara's face, the Buddha invited the demon inside for tea.

Don't get me wrong—the Buddha didn't send special invitations to Mara, or make up the guest bedroom. But he figured: so long as you're here, we might as well sip some soothing oolong and get to know each other. In doing so, the Buddha found a way to embrace his entire life, including the parts he didn't like.

If we only welcome the stuff we like, there's a whole other aspect of our existence we don't even recognize, let alone claim. Our riverbed becomes dammed, and the life inside can't flow or thrive.

By inviting Mara to tea, we tell life that we care about it—and not just parts of it, but all of it.

Well-being is not based on who shows up at our door. It's based on how we treat them: do we invite them in, or shut them out in the cold?

OPENING THE DOOR

TO DEPRESSION

Depression runs in my family. From a relatively young age, I found myself slipping into psychological states that overwhelmed me. My emotions were raw, like exposed nerve endings, and hopelessness threw a dark shade over everything.

When depression showed up at my door, I did not invite it in. I *slammed* the door in its face, and probably threw in a one-fingered gesture for good measure.

In other words, I picked up my weapons and resisted life. Here were a few blades I kept sharp for such an occasion:

- I shamed myself for feeling depressed.

- I pretended like everything was fine when it wasn't.

- I lashed out in my relationships.

- I numbed my experience with food and television.

These patterns were mostly unconscious. Some part of me believed that if I resisted enough, my depression would leave. Or if I *didn't* resist, it would *never* leave.

After my brother Scott died, when I started taking a closer look at my life, I realized how hard I was on myself. My depression wasn't my fault— it's never anyone's fault. But I *was* responsible for how I treated myself when I felt depressed, and my track record was not full of gold stars.

Once I learned about inviting Mara to tea, I started practicing. When depression showed up, I put a tight leash on my old habits and opened the door. Heart pounding, worried about the possible confrontation ahead, I said, "Hello, Depression. Why don't you come in?"

During that first visit, there were some long, awkward silences punctuated by slurping and clinking porcelain. I drummed my fingers on the table, still wishing Depression would just go away so I could return to my "normal" life.

But after a few visits, I realized this was still my life. There was no "normal," not really. And if Depression was going to keep coming back, I could be brave enough to ask it questions. *What's going on? Is there a reason you're visiting?* Sometimes it had answers, sometimes not. We slowly grew to know each other better.

More importantly, I started asking *myself* questions. I was accustomed to abandoning myself when Depression visited, as if I couldn't stand to be around that version of me. Now that I was allowing Depression inside, I tried offering myself support. *Is there anything you need, Laura?*

The requests that surfaced were simple, though not necessarily easy.

Be kind to yourself. Slow down.

I tried my best. I was surprised the answers weren't about making Depression leave. As if some inner part of me knew that although Depression's visits were out of my control, how I treated myself was not.

Over time, the most amazing thing happened. Depression stopped feeling like some doomsday event that indicated I was weak and deficient—that wasn't "supposed" to happen.

It just was.

It was one part of my life, at times painful, but when I stopped resisting, my suffering lessened. When I was in my riverbed of well-being,

Depression's heavy runoff might have made my waters swell, but I was still bigger than the deluge. Depression could flow *and* I could experience others things at the same time. Like worthiness, and love.

All life wants to be lived, including the challenging parts. If we chop off a few limbs because we don't like them, it doesn't make us stronger. Plus, those phantom limbs linger, and they'll pester us until we say *yes* to even them.

WELL-BEING

RECLAIMS ENERGY

Resisting life takes energy.

Do you feel it? That siphoning of internal resources to erect and maintain barriers between what is and what we think should be? It happens without our knowing.

Our co-worker completes their part of our joint project late and the pressure lands on us to get it finalized. We fume about it for three days, and simmer every time we see them. Or our haircutter takes off a few extra inches, even though we *told them* shoulder length, and we run frustrated fingers through it for weeks, willing it to grow faster.

When we add up all of our micro resistances, we have no energy left to be the person we want to be. We're too tired, too burnt out.

When we embrace life, our barriers crumble, and we suddenly have a cache of energy ready to be redirected. Do we want to put it towards practicing self-love? Towards becoming more present as a partner or parent? Towards establishing gentle but strong boundaries with others, so that we don't feel taken advantage of? It's amazing the answers that find us when we reclaim the energy currently feeding resistance. As if they were waiting there all along.

This is where our limitless potential lies. Not in muscling life into submission, but in opening to it fully and completely, like a powerful, yawning riverbed capable of holding anything.

It is through the complete acceptance of life that we find the energy to be the person we want to be.

FEARS, FLAWS,

AND HARRY POTTER

Sometimes we're afraid to embrace life as it is. We encounter hardships and limitations, and we decide it would be much easier to float in the river, bumping along and blaming life for the bruises inflicted by downed trees and submerged rocks. Never leaning into our discomfort. Never taking risks.

Writing books is frightening. I fear what people will say. I fear what I'll think a few years from now when I flip through these pages. Sharing something from a place of imperfection is vulnerable. Part of me wants to mitigate that risk and only share my creations when I'm perfect.

The trouble of course is that I'll never be perfect. I would spend my entire life waiting for an eventuality that would never come, sacrificing my dreams because of my fears and flaws.

There's a reason we love Harry Potter. Despite his fears and flaws, he still accepts his destiny and steps into the unknown. Harry isn't the most likely candidate to save the wizarding world. He's young, inexperienced, and at times brash. Heck, he's not even the most talented wizard in his class, let alone alive.

For a while, Harry would much rather someone else be "The Chosen One" and face the evil Lord Voldemort. Harry doesn't want to fight. He wants to live peacefully with his friends and family. But he can only avoid his life for so long, and Harry eventually realizes the consequences of *not* embracing his life are too high. He risks the lives of his friends and other innocents; he risks everything good in the world being wiped away by Voldemort's dark stain. Despite his fears and flaws, Harry must lean into his discomfort and say *yes* to life.

The millions of people who read Harry Potter thought they were escaping to another world. They didn't realize it was their own life they were captivated by. Harry's journey mirrors our own. The more we avoid life, as Harry tried to do, the more severe the consequences. If we're merely trying to get by unscathed, without leaning into life, we'll never know what we truly could have become.

We will always be flawed. We will always be a little afraid, a little uncertain if we'll be able to handle what comes our way. But those things shouldn't prevent us from thriving. Harry finally says *yes* to being The Chosen One, and in doing so, he discovers that his potential exceeds his limitations. He *can* handle what comes his way; he *can* overcome the odds.

Very few people get to the end of their life and wish they had resisted more. Instead, they wish they had honored their fears and flaws, and decided to act anyway. They wish they had published the book, gotten the degree, or forgiven the estranged parent.

Because it would have brought them closer to the life they wanted all along.

WELL-BEING IS ACTIVE

There's a common misconception that acceptance is passive. A throwing up of our hands and declaring, "I guess this is just my life. I'm an angry person—deal with it."

That's not well-being.

Well-being knows life isn't rigid, but constantly flowing. It leans into the mystery of each moment, wondering how we can respond uniquely with all the resources at our disposal. Well-being knows we have the capacity to be anyone we want to be, and that it is a very *active* choice.

WELL-BEING: AN EXAMPLE

My husband and I were at a dinner party with friends. They had family members in town, and after some pleasant conversation, our ideas started to clash.

Not normal ideas—very personal ideas. Experiences that meant a lot to us. People were getting emotional as tones grew sharp.

I could tell my husband was upset. His face was pinched, lips tight. There were tears in his eyes. Finally, he said, "I'm feeling really frustrated right now, and I think I need to leave." Everyone got quiet. I said my goodbyes and drove him home, knowing he was my priority, that things with our friends would be fine.

Curled up together on the couch, he started crying. "I'm so mad," he squeezed out. "I want to punch a wall or scream at someone."

I felt a bit stunned by what I was witnessing. Though he couldn't see it, he was practicing well-being. His muscles were trembling, emotions storming, and yet he had been able to express his feelings and state his needs.

He was in his riverbed, even as large logs dominated his waters.

Well-being didn't make those logs smaller, or any less brutal as they scarred his banks. It didn't lessen his pain. But well-being made it possible for him to choose who he wanted to be in that moment, and to minimize damage to himself and others.

Well-being made it possible for him to have his authentic experience, and to also be bigger than it.

Later that night, his big reaction had floated past, and he was able to objectively reflect on what happened. "I can understand what they said, and why they felt that way," he said. "I respect them. I don't know why I got so upset." He was a little embarrassed, but even that he allowed.

When we allow life, intense experiences pass more quickly. If we aren't expending energy trying to stop the logs from being there in the first place, they float past on their own. Life naturally likes to flow, and though it can be uncomfortable, if we remain in our riverbed during the turbulence, we can maintain a slightly bigger perspective, without judgment.

My, this is quite the storm. I wonder how long it will last.

IT'S OKAY TO FORGET

It's hard to live in well-being all the time. I don't think many people achieve it. This is an imperfect practice, just as we are imperfect beings.

Here's how well-being usually goes for me: I remember well-being and life feels a little more easeful; then I forget and start resisting the parts of my life I don't like; then I remember and put down my weapons; then I'm faced with a new challenge and slap on my armor once more.

This is the dance of well-being—remembering, forgetting, remembering, forgetting.

Just today I was telling a girlfriend about my fears around sharing this book. "How can you let fear be a part of your process," she asked, "instead of pushing it away?"

Huh. Funny—not twenty minutes earlier, I had been writing about that same concept. Still, when confronted with a fresh wave of fears and insecurities, I forgot.

It's okay to forget. It doesn't make us unworthy of happiness. Over time—with practice—we remember well-being a little faster, like a muscle becoming toned. But regardless of how long it takes, the trick is to not shame ourselves for forgetting. We merely step back into our riverbed and gently embrace that forgetting is part of our journey. There's room for it, too.

WHAT WELL-BEING

REALLY WANTS

A meditation teacher dying from cancer woke up every morning and said, "Gratitude."

He then sat quietly and let his pains fill in the blank.

Gratitude. *Sore back*. Gratitude. *Exhaustion*.

Like anyone with a terminal illness, he wouldn't have chosen that path, but because it was his reality, he decided to work with it.

That's all well-being asks. That we work with the life we have. That we don't abandon this moment as if there were something better if we fought hard enough to get it.

There is only here. Now. And if we allow it, it can be everything we want.

BOOK TWO

WELL-BEING AND US

Who Are We, Really?

A girl should be two things:
who and what she wants.

−Coco Chanel

A ROADMAP

If you're like me, your relationship with yourself is complicated. Sure, there are moments of love, but there are also hidden stories of inadequacy, judgment, and shame. Some days you feel like you're poised at the edge of the world, and other days you feel completely lost, like you don't even know who you are.

One of the most challenging places to embrace life is in our relationship with ourselves. And yet this is arguably where we need well-being the most.

I'd like to start by pulling back the curtain on one of the most intimate parts of our existence: our thoughts. That mental activity that's with us all day long. And, if we aren't paying attention, is subtly ruling us.

From there, we'll tackle the big kahuna, the part of ourselves we take very, very personally.

Our identity.

It's a lot to unpack. This is sensitive territory. Let's add a dash of gentleness as we move forward into well-being and us.

WHAT ARE THOUGHTS?

Thoughts. That endless stream of mental chatter, sometimes providing useful information, other times trolling our heads with hangry, half-formed opinions.

Have you ever tried observing your thoughts, as if you were watching a movie reel play across the screen of your mind? They have some odd characteristics.

In some form or another, our thoughts are always there. They have no discernible beginning or end—they typically jump in somewhere in the middle, and are replaced by another thought before reaching a conclusion. They're challenging to control, and sometimes express things we don't agree with, as if they had a mind of their own.

Some mindfulness teachers use the term "monkey mind" to describe our default mode of thinking. The image is perfect—a troop of wild monkeys romping through our heads, swinging on branches and flinging poop while singing "I

Wanna Be Like You." Not because they're bad, but because that's what monkeys *do*. They're curious, tireless, and usually untrained.

This, however, is not to underestimate our thoughts. They can be powerful; powerful enough to shape our reality. And if we aren't careful, we might even believe them.

WHERE DO THOUGHTS

COME FROM?

At a workshop with meditation teacher Jack Kornfield, he told us to close our eyes and count how many thoughts we had over the course of thirty seconds.

As I did so, I was amazed that some of my thoughts were words and others impressions, like a "knowing." Some felt like small drops of emotion beading across my mind, and others danced like flames flickering in and out of my consciousness. My number was somewhere in the 20's. *Twenty thoughts in thirty seconds?!* By a show of hand, almost everyone in the room had a large number of thoughts. It was comforting to know I wasn't the only one.

But where did they come from? What created my thoughts, different from the people next to me? And why were they sometimes unpleasant?

Thoughts are mysterious. What they are, where they come from, why we have them we can't entirely know. But science has revealed a few things about thoughts that can help us better understand this phenomenon.

One place thoughts originate is other thoughts. Neuroscientists use the analogy of a wagon wheel rolling along a muddy road. The more the wheel repeats that journey, the deeper the tracks become, and the more likely the wheel is to follow the established rut. In our brains, the more we think a thought, the stronger that neural connection becomes, and the more likely we are to think it again. Our past thoughts are impacting what we're thinking right now, and what we're thinking right now is impacting future thoughts.

Thoughts also come from influences around us. Have you ever had a thought that sounded just your dad, as if he spoke straight into your head, and you finally realized, "Ah, *that's* where that thought comes from."

Our families, the media we consume, our workplace—the messaging around us shapes how we think. Which is why my husband gave me a disapproving look when I started watching *Game of Thrones* and asked, "Are you sure? Trash in, trash out." (The story of course ends with him sitting beside me every week, enthusiastically singing the theme song while riding an imaginary horse.)

Understanding where thoughts come from can help us separate *what we think* from *who we are*. Despite being in our head, thoughts actually aren't that personal. They're more like the byproduct of a neurological process that feeds off of everything it comes in contact with.

Thus, it's quite possible that our thoughts have been shaped by everything else.

That isn't to diminish the influence thoughts can have over us. Our perception creates our reality, and thoughts are a big part of the equation.

THE THOUGHTS WE BELIEVE

CREATE OUR REALITY

_____

Growing up, my thoughts created a negative reality. And oh, it felt very real. I believed I was unintelligent and unlovable, even when there was a surplus of evidence to the contrary. That's how convincing thoughts can be—they alter how we take in information, ignoring data that might undermine them. (It doesn't have to be downplayed thoughts. We all know someone who believes they are the *most* intelligent, and the *most* lovable, despite possible evidence to the contrary!)

I didn't know why I had these thoughts (ahem: *everything else*), but my reality felt inescapable. I believed it was my lot in life—that I was not destined to be an easygoing, happy person, even though I appeared that way on the outside.

"What an interesting thought," my Zen teacher, Flint Sparks, once said to me on a retreat after I shared some of my darker beliefs about myself.

"You know, you don't have to believe that if you don't want to."

"What do you mean?"

"Is that thought helpful?"

That was easy. "No. It hurts."

"Do you see any reason to keep it?"

"No. I'd like to learn how to love myself."

"Then you could say back to it, 'Thank you for visiting me, but I choose not to believe you.'"

A few moments passed.

" Then what?"

He shrugged. "Do that enough times and you might stop believing it. And then," he added, eyes sparkling, "you can choose which thoughts you *want* to believe."

MENTAL DIALOGUE

That tool my Zen teacher gave me—I took it literally. My thoughts and I have conversations.

For example, I might have the thought, "You haven't accomplished anything meaningful. What are you doing with your life?"

My first response, quite honestly, is *ouch*. But I take a moment to pause and remember that just because this thought surfaced doesn't make it true. In fact, it might not even be my thought!

Then I say back to it, as if we were having a stimulating dinner conversation, "That's interesting, but I actually don't agree with you. I *have* accomplished meaningful things." I might even laugh lightly. Nothing dissolves negative self-talk like kind laughter.

The key is not to judge or get defensive, but to be gentle. Our mean thoughts don't come from a cruel place, but a frightened one. Some part of us is feeling vulnerable and tries to reestablish safety by inhibiting us from taking action.

When I received the email that I had been selected to give a TEDx talk, the first thought that passed through my mind was, "You will be the first speaker in the history of TED talks to forget your lines."

Thanks, brain.

Not the most helpful thought I could have had, but I knew it came from a frightened place. There was a part of me that feared failing, that feared being laughed at, and that part said those words to prevent me from putting myself in a vulnerable position. The only safe option it could conceive of was to stop me before I started.

It doesn't work to yell back at this part. She wants gentleness. She wants to be told that I appreciate her ideas and hear her requests, and though I love her, she doesn't get to decide how I live. Even if it scares her, we're getting on that TEDx stage, because it's important. And even if we forget our talk, it won't be the end of the world.

Self-love starts here—not in grand gestures, but in the small way we treat each thought. Each time we show a harsh thought kindness, we demonstrate an enormous expression of self-love.

In doing so, we start living the life we want in this moment.

CHOOSING NEW THOUGHTS

Our brains are flexible. Although not always easy, we can encourage our wagon wheel down different muddy paths, strengthening new thoughts and letting old ones dry up, maybe even fill in with time.

Every morning I read a piece of paper taped to my wall titled "My Contract with the Universe." It's a list my life goals and steps for accomplishing them, and also a list of the thoughts I want to foster. "Trust yourself," I read out loud each morning while facing east, because it feels auspicious, "and enjoy living *your* life, no one else's."

The more I read my contract, the more my pre-approved thoughts deepen in their tracks. The amazing thing is I find myself actually thinking them later in the day, usually when facing a challenge. "You support Adrian on *his* journey, not yours, and cultivate love, acceptance, and appreciation for all that he is," I remind myself when my husband loudly strums his *un*tuned guitar beside me while I'm reading. (Did I mention he doesn't actually know how to play, just likes strumming random things?)

We can't always control the thoughts we think. They're like leaves on a towering cottonwood tree beside our riverbed. When the wind blows, hundreds twirl through the air and land in our water, whether we want them to or not. But we can train how we respond to our thoughts. Do we get lost in their content, or are we able to offer that kind laughter?

Silly thought. What a funny thing to think.

IDENTITY

Changing my relationship to my thoughts is one of the most powerful tools I've learned. It has made my mental space a little tidier, a little easier to navigate. With the new space, there's room for more joy to arise.

But there's another relationship I've worked on, though not without some difficulty. One that impacts my life in even bigger ways.

My identity.

It all began with the question: *am I really who I think I am?*

WHO WE THINK WE ARE

Years ago, the Dalai Lama was meeting with Western meditation teachers. One asked the Dalai Lama how he worked with self-hatred.

The Dalai Lama turned to his translator, confused. He knew a fair amount of English, but this last word wasn't coming through. After a few exchanges, the Dalai Lama finally looked around the group and said, "This is a mistake!"

There was no comparable word for self-hatred in Tibetan, and even the concept seemed foreign. The Dalai Lama couldn't understand why someone would hate themselves.

Each culture faces unique challenges. For some of us in Western society, self-judgment, high expectations, and self-criticism are embedded from the start. These are areas where I've had to set down my weapons, brew some tea, and start asking questions.

Was I really unworthy of love? Was I really destined to be unhappy, never satisfied with who

I was? Where did my ideas about myself come from?

We rarely question the authority of our identity—of who we think we are. Why would we? No one wakes up one day and *decides* they're unworthy of love. It just feels like truth. Like some objective reality.

But there is no objective reality. And our identities, as personal as they feel, are nothing more than subjective opinions.

The great thing about opinions is we can change them.

IS THAT TRUE?

While backpacking around Southeast Asia at 23, wondering if I'd "find myself" on a remote trek in the Himalayas, I read a book by Byron Katie called *Loving What Is*. In it, Katie establishes a series of questions that challenge the stories we tell ourselves about who we are.

The first question is, "Is it true?" *Is it true that I'm not intelligent? Is it true that I haven't done anything with my life?*

And just in case the answer is a hand flipping back and forth with an uncertain *Well* , the second question is, "Can I absolutely know that it's true?" That one always cuts through the crap. We can never *absolutely* know that our subjective opinions of ourselves are true.

Asking questions like these requires bravery. We've likely believed our stories for years, maybe our entire lives. Doing so can be uncomfortable. Destabilizing. If I've identified as a sensitive person, what does it mean if I stop responding emotionally to things? If I identify as independent, what does it mean if I start opening up to support from others?

But Katie poses one final question, and it helps relieve that shakiness. In fact, it might just be the most powerful question we can ask ourselves: "Who would I be without that thought?"

Answer: anyone you want.

IDENTITY LOSS

When my brother Scott died, I felt a secondary loss that was hard to name, even harder to describe.

It was the loss of an identity.

In a household that was at times tumultuous, the only security I felt growing up was in my role as a sister. I was good at it. It was uncomplicated. I followed Scott around, supporting his ideas and playing his games, and was rewarded with attention and love. My identity as a sister was like a gravitational force. It drew me to him, but also to a place inside myself where I trusted that I belonged.

Even into college, that part of my identity remained important at a time when much of who I was felt in question. When he died, there was a gaping hole where he used to be, but also where *I* used to be. At least, where I believed my greatest worth resided.

Sister. I was a sister.

Without that, who was I?

It's like parents becoming empty nesters when so much of their identity was tied to raising their children. Or when a college graduate must become a "grown up." Or when a relationship ends and we don't know who we are without that person.

None of this is bad. We don't need to rip away our identities because they're somehow wrong or make us weak. If anything, our identities make us feel safe in a life that's always a little unstable; a life that makes us wonder if we're doing it right, or if the next best thing is just around the corner.

Still, it's useful to realize that although our subjective identities might mean a great deal to us, they're like boulders in our river, not the riverbed itself. And if we're tired of holding on, we can let them go.

WHY AM I THIS WAY?

I was walking with a friend by, funny enough, a river. She told me she was working on her feelings of unworthiness. "It's hard. I'm so used to saying, 'Why am I this way? What's wrong with me?'"

I could relate. Some of our beliefs about ourselves run deep. They're the undertow in our riverbed, stealthy and strong, dragging things down with a rough tug.

We take life personally, but is it? Like our thoughts, is our identity solely a product of *us*?

We didn't get to choose our families or how we were raised. We didn't get to choose how our friends talked about body image around us, or how our teachers defined success.

Who we are has been shaped by innumerable influences inside and outside of our control. Even we can't identify them all. So when we ask, "Why am I this way?" the answer is because of a lot of other stuff. And when we criticize ourselves by saying, "What's wrong with me?" we aren't being fair.

Certain parts of our lives aren't our fault. We can take the burden of blame off our shoulders.

But here's the thing: life is still our responsibility.

Our wounds aren't our fault, but we're responsible for how we treat them. Our negative thoughts aren't our fault, but we're responsible for which thoughts we encourage.

Instead of asking, "Why am I this way?" we can ask, "How am I becoming the person I want to be with the life I've been given?"

NO ONE SPECIAL TO BE

About four years back, while flipping through a Buddhist magazine, I encountered an article titled "No One Special to Be."

It caught my interest, but in a defensive way. As a young professional, I was working hard to "be someone." To prove myself, to be important, to have a core mission that was unique and meaningful and attention-grabbing.

I took personal offense at the idea of being "no one special," so I angry-read the article. As the sentences passed, the strangest feeling washed over me. In the span of three innocent pages, my entire identity was thrown into question, and I felt myself traversing the stages of a kind of grief. By the end, a weight lifted off my very being; a weight I had no idea I'd been carrying.

My desire to be clearly defined in the world created pervasive, low-level anxiety. Each moment I spent not being "someone" fed my resistance towards life. *If I can just figure this out, then I'll feel secure in who I am!*

But maybe, as this author suggested, I had been going about it the wrong way. If I actually *let go* of my search for a solid identity—if I had "no one special to be"—I could just *be*

And I could still do what I loved, but without the pressure of labels or status to feel safe. I would have nothing to prove, to myself or others.

Something about that tasted like freedom.

IS ALADDIN REALLY

A STREET RAT?

Or, in the words of Aladdin:
"Riff raff, street rat, I don't buy that/ If only they'd look closer/ Would they see a poor boy?/ No siree; they'd find out there's so much more to me."

And you. There's so much more to *you*.

Beyond your circumstances, beyond your history, beyond your DNA and your family and your thoughts and your actions.

Why would you ever limit yourself to something as small as an identity, when, if you let identity *go*, you could choose who you want to be in every moment?

CHOOSING USEFUL

IDENTITIES

O nce I learned I didn't have to believe my thoughts about myself, I felt like Jim Carry's character in *The Truman Show* when he discovers his life is a TV show and he finally joins the world outside.

Freedom. Liberation. An expansive view of my life that, now that I had it, I couldn't go back.

But there was a missing piece. I didn't want to have *no* identity. There were parts of myself I loved. Parts that were curious, generous, forgiving, theatrical, feminine, empathetic, playful. How could I be free of my identities but still be *me*?

This was the critical distinction I needed: well-being isn't about abandoning all identities, but choosing *useful* identities.

It's amazing how many of our harmful identities rely on our lack of investigation. As soon as we start shining a light on the negative stories we tell ourselves, curiously leaning in with a giant magnifying glass and trench coat, a lot of them dissolve pretty quickly.

They aren't entirely gone. This isn't the work of a few days, but a lifetime. We'll find ourselves telling negative stories again because they're familiar, and old habits die hard. But with time and effort—slowly, surely—we'll start chipping away at identities that are no longer useful to us. And we'll start embracing ones that are.

Whenever I notice an identity that isn't useful resurfacing, I ask, "Who would I be without that thought?"

USEFUL IDENTITIES,

LIGHTLY HELD

U seful identities are, well, *useful*, but if we cling to them, they become rigid, and we're back where we started.

Can we hold them lightly, too?

RIVERBED OF IDENTITY

At the end of the day identity is a mental construct. Anything that takes language to express or requires concepts to understand is inherently limited.

But who we are, who we truly are, is limitless.

In each moment, we have the opportunity to generate a completely unique response to what's happening and how we perceive it. In each moment, we can cast aside our self-limiting beliefs, the stories of *who we think we are*, and carve out a different path.

Well-being invites us into our riverbed, the one that unlocks us from our internal boxes of "identity" and releases us into the realm of boundless potential.

BOOK THREE

WELL-BEING AND OTHERS

Intimacy in Relationships

When we feel love and kindness towards others,
it not only makes others feel loved and cared for,
but it helps us also to develop
inner happiness and peace.

—The Dalai Lama

WELL-BEING AND OTHERS

Five years after Scott died, I was working on a memoir about my journey with grief, and I was struggling.

I wanted to connect with other people who were experiencing grief—other sisters and family members and friends. I didn't have answers. I probably didn't have the most insightful reflections. I just wanted to tell my story as a way to say, "I know it hurts—you aren't alone."

Draft after draft, I wrote and deleted. Words were coming, but they weren't the right ones. It seemed so permanent, putting something in print, and every time I thought I had it, it slipped away, mercurial and elusive. I was frustrated. My inability to tell my story felt like a failure to find clarity about my own life.

Then a different idea came. I'm not entirely sure how it happened. Maybe it was something my husband said offhandedly, or maybe Scott planted it in a dream.

A live performance, I decided one day. *I'll do a live, one-woman play about my journey with grief, and then host a discussion with audiences.*

It seemed a bit bizarre, even to me. Who would want to see a one-woman show about grief? Who would want to *talk* afterwards?

But something was calling, and its voice was loud, like Scott's. We had done theatre together growing up, and it only seemed right to start again as a way to connect with others through loss.

On the evening of my first performance, I was so nervous I sweat through my shirt before I began, the dark stains under my arms impossible to miss. A friend had helped me procure two standing lights, and we created a small stage in a community center run by another friend. My opening sequence was shaky, but as the performance continued and I relaxed enough to pay attention, I noticed something was happening.

That connection I'd hoped to have with readers through my memoir it became a living, breathing relationship with the audience before me. The story may have been based on my life, but audience members were experiencing their own stories at the same time. Memories and emotions flitted behind their eyes. It was personal, yet communal—through our tears and laughter and the feeling that maybe something as individual as grief was in fact shared.

Afterwards, we circled our chairs and passed around a talking stick. Some people told their stories of loss, and others gave a nod or a word of thanks. Some mentioned parts of the performance that resonated with them, while others thanked strangers for previous comments, or shared what's helped them on their journey with grief.

People made eye contact, seeing one another in a way we don't often see those around us—with attentive, loving presence. And in that room of concrete and bright colors, we all healed a little together.

LIFE IS BIG

———————

Before creating my one-woman performance, even though I had spent years writing my memoir, it felt like there was an itch I couldn't quite scratch. Like I was missing some crucial part of my grieving process.

It wasn't until I stood on stage that I identified it: I hadn't been sharing my story with others. I hadn't been tapping into the vast capacity for human connection to support my healing journey. And a Word document just didn't cut the mustard.

Thus far we've focused on well-being as a solitary journey. Our society often promotes the individual, both when celebrating someone's success as wholly theirs, but also when declaring our problems to be solely ours to address—that we need to "fix" ourselves.

Though our work as individuals is important, we actually can't do this alone. We aren't *designed* to do it alone. We're meant to engage with the relational nature of our lives, and to find well-being here, too.

Life is big. Whether it's our joys or pains, our experiences are sometimes too big for one person to hold. When our happiness overflows, we want our loved ones to feel the runoff; to celebrate with us through weddings and baby showers and graduations.

Pain is the same. When our pain feels too big, we need someone to listen, to support us, to help carry the weight, if only for a moment.

Nothing amplifies our joys and eases our pains like sharing life with others.

RELATIONSHIPS CAN BE HARD

Despite their vast benefits, relationships can be hard.

Imagine two people coming together as partners. They've had two entirely different lives, comprised of infinitely different moments, and now they expect to get along most of the time. Throw in unclear communication, overwhelming emotions, the distractions of modern life, debris floating through their riverbeds

It's a miracle we even try.

When bringing two lives together, in friendship or partnership, it's helpful to remember that we're asking a lot. Can we be a little kinder? A little more understanding? Can we recognize that we too know what it feels like to cause unintentional harm?

We'll get it wrong at times. It's okay. That doesn't mean we should stop trying. Instead, maybe we could lean in further and ask ourselves

in each interaction: what can I learn from this
wisdom teacher in front of me?

WHAT WE REALLY WANT

One summer evening, I watched from the kitchen window as two boys played soccer in the grass park at the center of our neighborhood. One cried out, and I turned from chopping peppers to watch as the boy fell to the ground, holding his shin and curling to his side.

I wondered what the other boy would do. Call to the parents chatting on the surrounding sidewalk? Retrieve the ball that had skittered towards the community garden and ignore his friend out of anger or embarrassment?

He did neither. Instead, he went to his friend and sat on the grass beside him.

The injured one hurled a few half-hearted fists onto the other's shoulder—maybe it was deserved, maybe it wasn't. Either way, the friend took the blows, then remained sitting, offering his company. When the injured boy began to stand, his friend wandered off to collect the ball and passed it gently to the injured boy, who was now walking fine.

That's what we really want. For someone to sit beside us when we hurt. For them to forgive the thoughtless blows we deliver from our wounded, helpless state. Then for them to re-engage with us, not as broken people, but maybe with a little tenderness until we're fully recovered.

Never a hint of judgment. Never a question of whether or not we'll make it back into the game.

DO YOU CHOOSE ME?

In every interaction with another person, we ask three unconscious questions.

1. Do you see me?

2. Do you hear me?

3. Do you choose me, just as I am?

We all know what it feels like to be seen, heard, and chosen, just as we are and when we aren't. The former fosters warmth and belonging, the latter disconnect and loneliness.

I was at a retreat for entrepreneurs. As a creative, I felt out of place among founders and CEOs of successful companies, ranging from a design firm solving environmental problems to tech companies.

My insecurities persisted on the second day when we broke into small groups and shared our goals for our businesses, offering each person feedback. While others asked for advice on raising millions of dollars in capital, or encouraging systemic change in the World Bank, self-critical thoughts swirled. What were they going to say when I talked about preparing to give a TEDx talk about my performances on grief, or launching a book about well-being? Would they be able to tell how amateur I felt in comparison to their global reach?

When it was my turn to share, my judgmental thoughts dissolved as my group encouraged me with so much enthusiasm, tears welled. They said things like, "The work you're doing is so important—keep going!" and, "You've got this, don't be afraid to dream big."

It's not often that we experience this kind of supportive attention, or offer it to others. But that can change. Seeing, hearing, and choosing someone is both a presence we can embody, and literal words we can say. We can use them with our loved ones when they share something vulnerable. I said them to my husband as we laid on the couch that night after our friends' dinner. "I see you. I hear you. I choose you, just as you are."

When interacting with people we don't know well, we can convey the same messages by making eye contact, focusing on their story, and reflecting their worthiness back to them. "That sounds like a long day," I told a librarian the other night after she expressed how tired she was. "I hope you get some good sleep tonight. You've earned it."

If you want to be seen, heard, and chosen more in your life, you can specifically ask loved ones to provide that kind of attention. "I'd love to share something with you. I don't need you to fix anything or try to make me feel better. I'd just like you to see me, hear me, and choose me, just as I am."

Seeing, hearing, and choosing people is an expression of care. A small way in which we acknowledge that this person in front of us is a fellow human, and they deserve love and belonging, just as we do.

THE ART OF FORGIVING

There are plenty of times when we don't see people, or hear what they say, or choose them as they are.

That is to say, there are times when we cause harm, intentionally and unintentionally, knowingly and unknowingly. We're messy mammals, and we inevitably bump into each other as we move through the world. How can forgiveness become a part of well-being, too?

My husband and I had a rough first year of marriage. We didn't know how to communicate with each other, and when we felt vulnerable, our words came out wrong. After a number of poorly conducted arguments, we discovered a protocol we could follow. It's a Hawaiian practice of reconciliation called "Ho'oponopono," which means, "to make right." The phrases are, "I'm sorry. Please forgive me. Thank you. I love you."

After causing harm, whether it was intended or not, we come together by speaking those phrases, slowly and with heart. *I'm sorry. Please forgive me. Thank you. I love you.*

The part about intentionality is important. There are plenty of times when we act with good intentions, but still cause someone harm. It doesn't mean we're bad people, nor does it make the other person's reaction wrong. We're responsible for the impacts of our actions, just as much as our intentions, and we can ask for forgiveness when we misstep.

The amazing thing about forgiveness is it benefits the person doing the forgiving even more than the person being forgiven. There are times when we'll never talk to someone again, but we can still forgive them in our hearts—not to condone their behavior, but to finally release that weight, for our own sake.

Although it can be hard to open our hearts after we've been hurt, that's one of the beautiful aspects of being human. That we can heal. That we can forgive. That we can learn to love again, and in doing so, we are uplifted into better versions of ourselves, together.

SOME RELATIONSHIPS END

O ne of my favorite meditation practices is called "metta," or "loving kindness." It is the thoughtful offering of kind wishes to others, both people we find easy to love and struggle to love.

Metta tenderizes the heart. It primes us to feel love, even if it's not our default mode. To see the good in others, even if we're easily defensive or critical.

I use metta when faced with challenges in relationships, and also to transition out of relationships that have ended. Whether with a previous boyfriend or the natural ending of high school friendships, I quietly offer that person good wishes, and thank them for all that they were to me.

Especially as a people-pleaser, it's easy to feel like none of my relationships should end; that I should remain friends with everyone, always. But this isn't a practical way to move through life, and if we keep hanging on to people who supported us in the past but don't help our evolution going forward, then we can't progress.

There is grief in lost relationships, even if nothing "happened" to cause their end. By offering people love and good wishes—and thanking them—we can find closure within ourselves, and also honor that part of our life, as it led to who we are today.

SNAP JUDGMENTS,

HIDDEN DEPTHS

Our subconscious mind is responsible for processing a lot of information about the world around us. It also provides quick, gut reactions to stimuli we encounter.

This is helpful when a car is drifting into our lane, but it's not always helpful when meeting new people. Snap judgments can perpetuate stereotypes and biases. When we rely on our quick assumptions, we bypass the critical thinking part of our brain, and in doing so, we can make incorrect judgments, or at least incomplete ones.

Well-being, on the other hand, fosters curiosity about the people around us. It recognizes that we all have rich, unseen depths, and it suspends judgment in favor of connection.

I was recently reminded of this by a neighbor who stopped by my home office. My first response, even before opening the door, was irritation. I tend to get a bit cranky when people stop by my office unexpectedly. It disrupts my *flow*—or so my inflexible brain thinks.

He dropped something off for my husband, and instead of being on his way, he started asking questions about what I do. We had socialized at a few cookouts, but nothing of substance. I didn't think we had much in common.

After I explained my books and performance, he started telling me about his own experience with grief when, a few years back, he had a traumatic brain injury. The recovery process had been painful, he said, and not just physically. At one point, he planned to end his life, and was saved by the unconditional love of his dog. Even now, he sighed, some days were better than others.

Listening, I felt those shackles of judgment unlock. This was a person whom I'd seen smile easily and laugh heartily, and despite the pain in his story, he was still willing to open towards life, and to support others going through similar experiences.

I was reminded of how little we know about the people we pass. How we each contain multitudes, but we often forget, especially if we judge someone based on the stories *we* carry. I had put this person into a box based on my preconceived judgments, when in reality, he possessed so much more complexity and resilience than I had acknowledged.

It seemed like a tragedy that I hadn't taken the time before that moment to honor this person. That I hadn't truly recognized him as a *whole* person, even if I didn't know his story. How would it feel if we walked through the world with that intention in our hearts? To be generous in our assumptions of others. To suspend judgment and foster curiosity and compassion.

Not because we need to befriend everyone, but because kindness costs us nothing, and yet it can mean everything.

BELIEVING IN OTHERS

I have a passion for helping people tell their stories, which I do as a professional editor and ghost writer. Stories are valuable. They have the power to connect us, to help us grow, to support us in our healing. Stories allow us to express things we have a hard time talking about, but are nonetheless important to who we are.

Everyone has a story.

At some point in the process of writing their books, my clients always ask me, "Will anyone care?" Will anyone care about their traumas from the military, or how they learned to become a good father without a male role model?

I get it. We look to others for validation because it makes us feel secure. Yes, it's important to validate ourselves, but it's okay to want validation from others, too. That's how we learned what validation felt like in the first place. Because someone gave it to us.

It only takes one person to tell us *keep going* before we step outside our comfort zone and into the life we want. Some of the same people who asked me, "Will anyone care?" have gone on to publish bestsellers, launch far-reaching podcasts, even start a family foundation providing college scholarships to underserved youth. These incredible people still needed someone to believe in them, as we all do.

When I'm facing a new challenge, I find myself quietly looking to a loved one for reassurance. Not because I need their permission or approval, but because it reminds me: I am loved, I am seen, and no matter how this turns out, I am worthy.

I even asked my husband before publishing this book, "I know the answer to this question, but I'd still like to hear you say it. Will you still love me if this book turns out to be crap?"

He gave me a warm hug and laughed a bit in his chest. "Of course. I will love you even then." It was nice to be reminded. It was the boost I needed to face my fears, to be the person I wanted to be.

One of the best things we can do for others is see their boundless potential. That ineffable, foundational part of them beneath their stories and habits and thoughts.

Their riverbed of well-being.

And maybe, the more we see the potential in others, the more we'll see it in ourselves.

BOOK FOUR

THE MAGIC OF WELL-BEING

Beyond the Riverbed

Tell me, what is it you plan to do
with your one wild and precious life?

−Mary Oliver

THE HERO OF YOUR STORY

You might be familiar with the storytelling template of the hero's journey, which goes something like this:

A hero is living an ordinary life in an ordinary world, when suddenly, they are confronted by an enormous challenge. In order to overcome that challenge, they must adventure into the extraordinary world, where, through trials and tests, the hero gains new skills to aid their victory. Finally, they return to the ordinary world, but are forever changed by what transpired.

Everyone wants to be the hero of their story. To step into that extraordinary world and be transformed, returning empowered.

When we consider the portrayal of most heroes' journeys, they can be misleading. Most of us wouldn't voluntarily swap places with even the mildest of Disney characters, whose trials might include being orphaned at a young age, swallowed by a whale and shot out of its blowhole, or selling one's soul to a sea witch to endure what I can only imagine is the excruciating process of growing legs.

Fortunately, our transformations don't need to be that extreme. In fact, in every single moment, we have the capacity to step into the extraordinary world—into the realm of possibility that is our riverbed of well-being.

Our hero's journey is not about becoming flawless, but creating a little more space to accept our messiness. We welcome all of life's experiences because our power resides in choosing how we respond to what's happening, not forcing life to be something it isn't.

My Zen teacher often asks, "How simple are you willing to let this be?"

Sometimes life feels complicated, but not necessarily because it *is* complicated. More often than not, it's because we complicate what's simple.

We don't have to fight life. When we step out of the chaotic flow of our river and into our riverbed, we might discover we have far more energy to engage with life than we realized. Energy to be creative in how we show up each day; to be imaginative in how we resolve conflict; to be generous in our assumptions of others; to be thoughtful in choosing useful identities. To witness the awe and magic right before our eyes.

When we stop resisting life and allow it to simply *be*, we can access the wholeness that is already there, waiting for us.

Waiting for us to say *yes* and step into the extraordinary nature of this moment.

EVERY STORY ENDS

Even as a hero, our story eventually comes to an end. We know that no one ultimately survives this adventure. And though it can be uncomfortable, acknowledging our mortality can serve as a compass for life.

I see death as a call to action. If life is our most precious gift, then we have a responsibility to be a good steward of it. Of this body. Of this mind. Of these relationships. Of this experience. No one can live for us. It's up to us to optimize each of our remaining breaths, for they are finite and irreplaceable.

If we didn't have death, we'd have no reason to set down our weapons and *live*. Live this life. Not someone else's. Not the next one. We only have *this* life, and it doesn't ask for anything in return. Still, it would be nice to try—to try and be kind to ourselves and others. To try and stop resisting, or thinking life should be different when it's already magical, exactly as it is.

FINDING YOUR MAGIC

I started this book by acknowledging that sometimes life is hard.

It's okay. I see you.

My hope is that some of the things in this book offer you a different way forward. A way to be gentle with yourself when things are hard, to forgive yourself when your habits of judgment or shame take over. A way to know that you are bigger than your experiences.

May well-being be the loving container inside of which you can welcome your life in its entirety. May it provide you with a feeling of new beginnings in every moment. And when the waters of your river are raging, may your riverbed provide a safe haven to rest as you wait out the storm.

You are worthy. You are whole. You belong here.

I believe in you, and I choose you, just as you are. Not because you are more special than anyone else, but because you're *you*. And you're the only one of you that will ever exist.

Life is rare. It is fleeting, and it is precious. It's not always *easy*, but we still have a chance to choose our riverbed of well-being—to cultivate lasting happiness—as a way to honor this incredible opportunity we've been given.

I hope your journey continues to be filled with surprise and delight, but most of all, with love. That, to me, is where we find our magic. In our love and gratitude for all that we have in these ever-changing moments.

Be well.

MEDITATIONS

BASIC SITTING MEDITATION

This is a basic sitting meditation you can do each morning, or when you feel overwhelmed and want to step back into your riverbed of well-being. The key to practicing meditation is to start small, with achievable goals. Try five minutes for a few weeks, and if you like it, keep going! Sitting meditation is a great tool for cultivating stillness in a life that doesn't stop moving.

Find a comfortable, quiet place to sit in a chair or on the ground. With a straight back, relax your belly and arms, and gently close your eyes.

Take a few moments to settle in, noticing the sounds around you, the temperature of the room, and the feeling of your body being pulled to the earth. Scan your body from head to toe and notice how you're feeling.

Now, bring your attention to your breath. You might notice how your chest rises and falls with each inhale and exhale, or you might notice the brush of air inside your nostrils. Choose a sensation on which to focus, and observe your breath as it naturally moves in and out of your body.

If your mind wanders, acknowledge that you started thinking, and gently bring your attention back to your breath.

Continue the practice for your desired amount of time. When you're finished, softly blink your eyes open and take a few moments to reorient yourself in the room. Then, with a bit more space to embrace life, return to your day.

LOVING KINDNESS MEDITATION

Metta, or loving kindness meditation, is a beautiful way to practice self-love, and to soothe grievances you're holding in your heart. The practice consists of a series of phrases we offer to different people, wishing them well. Feel free to adjust the phrases to your liking. Notice how we start and end the practice by offering ourselves loving kindness, because if we aren't filled up, we can't effectively give to others.

Find a quiet, comfortable place to sit, and close your eyes. Take a few breaths to center yourself, letting all distractions and to-dos fall away.

Now, bring your attention to yourself. You can place a hand on your heart or focus on the feeling of your body. With love and kindness, slowly offer yourself these wishes:

May I be happy. May I be at peace. May I be free from suffering.

Take a deep breath, and exhale.

Next, bring to mind someone you love. Hold a picture of them in your head, and feel the warmth inside as you think of them. Slowly offer them these wishes, with love and kindness:

May you be happy. May you be at peace. May you be free from suffering.

Take a deep breath, and exhale.

Next, bring to mind someone you don't know that well, and with whom you have a neutral relationship. It might be someone you pass regularly, but you haven't talked to. Holding a picture of them in your head, slowly offer these wishes, with love and kindness:

May you be happy. May you be at peace. May you be free from suffering.

Take a deep breath, and exhale.

Next, bring to mind someone with whom you're having a challenging time. Maybe there's a wound that has yet to heal. Holding a picture of them in your head, slowly offer these wishes, with love and kindness:

May you be happy. May you be at peace. May you be free from suffering.

Take a deep breath, and exhale.

Now, imagine the entire world, and all beings. With love and kindness in your heart, slowly offer these wishes:

May all beings everywhere be happy. May all beings everywhere be at peace. May all beings everywhere be free from suffering.

Take a deep breath, and exhale.

Finally, return to yourself. Place a hand on your heart and offer these wishes once more, with love and kindness:

May I be happy. May I be at peace. May I be free from suffering.

Feel the warmth of your wishes seeping into your body, nourishing you even as they go out into the world. When you're ready, gently open your eyes.

A PRACTICE FOR STRESS

Pranayama is a yogic breath work practice. There are many types of pranayama, and they each have different benefits. It is well researched that controlled breathing helps calm the sympathetic nervous system, which is responsible for our fight/flight/freeze response. When we feel our heart rate spike and our anxiety kick in, that's our sympathetic nervous system at work. This breathing practice, called "alternate nostril breathing," is my favorite for calming my system when I'm stressed. Even if I'm not stressed, it's a peaceful way to start the day.

Find a comfortable place to sit with a straight back. Allow your belly to be relaxed and let one hand rest in your lap.

Bring your other hand to your nose with your thumb hovering by one nostril, and your middle finger by the other.

With your eyes closed, plug one nostril with your thumb as you inhale slowly and steadily for a count of five. At the top of your inhale, release that nostril and plug the other one with your middle finger, exhaling slowly and steadily for a count of five. Feel free to adjust your number, but keep your inhale and exhale even.

Continue breathing, alternating which nostril is plugged as you inhale and exhale. Repeat for a few minutes, or until you feel your body calm.

ACKNOWLEDGEMENTS

I wouldn't be who I am today without the incredible people who have supported me and loved me on my messy journey. The same can be said for this book.

First, to Flint Sparks, my Zen teacher, to whom this book is dedicated. You are one of the most generous people I know, and you have given me so much over the years. Thank you for saying "yes" to the role of teacher, for you benefit so many. And thank you for saying "yes" to me whenever I need support navigating the shaky parts of my life. You have helped me remove barriers to love, and I'm so deeply grateful.

To the other wisdom teachers from whom I've learned and with whom I've sat: Jack Kornfield, Tara Brach, Norman Fischer, Jon Kabat-Zin, Richard Schwartz, Byron Katie, and Michael Stone (we miss you so). You have all made an indelible impression on my life and heart. Thank you.

To my early readers: Aristotle Johns, Kelly Landau, Hilary Novacek Bundt, Laura Deloatch,

Emily Moody, and Kristy Wessel. Thank you all for the sage advice, and for helping this book be better than it could have been on its own. Thank you for the conversations about titles and river, for the little scribbled hearts, and for the encouragement. I love you all.

To Marité, my mentor and friend. So much of what I've learned over the years about gentleness is thanks to you. You are an embodiment of the divine feminine to which I aspire. I'm so grateful for your support in helping me flourish, and for the endless compassion you show me, no matter what!

To my parents: thank you for believing in me, for encouraging me, and for providing me with the final pep talk I needed to get this book out. You both have taught me what it means to be strong, and to put family first. I love you both, and I wouldn't be able to do this without you.

To Paula and Roger: thank you for being the best in-laws and for making me feel so loved and welcomed into the family (now that I've attended a Packers game). I couldn't imagine better champions on my side. I love you dearly.

To my husband, Adrian. My first and last reader; the peanut butter to my jelly; the one who picks me up again and again when I'm down and celebrates my wins with as many bags of chips and silly dances as I want. Thank you for cooking countless meals and cleaning up so I could keep writing. Thank you for showing me what well-being looks like in a marriage, and for being my best friend. You might have been the first author in the house, but you certainly aren't the last. I love you.

Finally, thank *you*, dear reader, for picking up this book with its bubblegum pink cover and my own magical take on life. I can't tell you how meaningful it is to make something and have it be seen, heard, and chosen in the world, as it was by you. I am forever grateful, and I hope we can continue the conversation, encouraging each other deeper into our riverbed of well-being.

Laura Thomas is an award-winning storyteller and writer who is dedicated to exploring our human journey. In her 2019 TEDx talk, she elevates the power of walking with our grief. She's also the writer, director, and performer of *Who Am I Without You?*, a one-woman performance about the loss of her brother. She lives in the mountains of Colorado with her husband, where she tells stories and helps others tell theirs inside a wasabi-colored house filled with crystals and a unicorn named Shadowfax.

www.LauraThomasWrites.com

Instagram: @laurathomaswrites

Made in the USA
Monee, IL
18 December 2019

19103680R00079